FAITH JOURNAL

by

Cynthia Owen

Faith Journal
ISBN: 978-0-9971652-1-0
Copyright © 2016 by Cynthia Owen

All rights reserved. No part of this book may be reproduced in any form without permission in writing from the publisher, except in the case of brief quotations embodied in critical articles or reviews.

All Scripture quotations are from the King James Version of the Bible.

Published by:
JC Owen and Associates, Inc.
3558 Round Barn Blvd., Suite 200
Santa Rosa, CA 95403

Printed in the United States of America.

Dear Friend,

Have you ever wondered how to understand faith? The Faith Journal was written to help you discover what faith is all about. Without faith it is impossible to please God, let alone receive anything from God.

I'm convinced that God is always trying to help us to increase our faith, encouraging us to believe Him for the kind of faith that can move a mountain.

I've learned that when all is going great, it's easy to believe God. But it's when times are tough that we really see just how strong our faith is in our lives.

Sometimes we just don't find ourselves in faith when we are wavering back and forth as our current circumstances change.

For many years I don't think I really understood what faith actually was or how it operated in our lives. I now have a simple word that I like to use when it comes to faith, and that's CONFIDENCE! Confidence is knowing God will be faithful to you and to what you are believing Him to do in your life.

The Faith Journal was created to help you understand faith so you can see what faith can do when you're believing God, and that applying the principles of faith to your own life can allow you to receive the promises that you are believing God for in your life. On the next page I have listed some of these faith truths to help you.

Each day as you write in your Faith Journal you will get a glimpse of the great men and women of faith and what they were able to accomplish through applying their FAITH!

Many blessings to you.

Cindy

KEYS TO BUILDING YOUR FAITH

Spend a lot of time in the word of God because it will build your faith and confidence. Romans 10:17 says, "So then faith cometh by hearing, and hearing by the word of God."

The Apostle Paul said, "Let this mind be in you, which was also in Christ Jesus ..." (Philippians 2:5). As you read the word of God, He will use His word to renew your mind.

Memorize the word of God. This, too, will renew your mind with right thinking. Your mind will call to remembrance those scriptures that you have memorized when you need them.

Learn to speak words of faith. God's word says in Proverbs 18:21 that "Death and life are in the power of the tongue: and they that love it shall eat the fruit thereof."

Call those things that you want to come to pass as if they already are, until those things are actually completed. Get into agreement with the word of God because He "calleth those things which be not as though they were." (Romans 4:17).

Prayer builds your faith. Learn to be in conversation with God throughout your day.

Use this Faith Journal to document the prayers that God is answering for you. This, too, will build your faith.

Get out on the waters of faith. Don't let fear hold you back. Step out in faith, because God promises to work with us in our journey of faith.

Know that God has already given faith to you. Romans 12:3 says, "... as God hath dealt to every man the measure of faith." Faith is **already in your heart**, and just waiting to be released into your life.

FAITH

"For we walk by faith, not by sight."
2 Corinthians 5:7

Insights:
_____
_____
_____
_____
_____
_____
_____
_____
_____
_____
_____
_____
_____
_____
_____
_____
_____
_____
_____

Faith

My Declaration: *"Lord, I declare that I will not look at my circumstances but **I will trust you** in everything I do in life."*

FAITH

*"Hope deferred maketh the heart sick:
but when the desire cometh, it is a tree of life."*
Proverbs 13:12

Insights:
_____
_____
_____
_____
_____
_____
_____
_____
_____
_____
_____
_____
_____
_____
_____
_____
_____
_____
_____
_____

Faith

My Declaration: *"Lord, I declare that I will continue to trust you **and I will not quit** until I see the promises that I am believing you for come to pass."*

FAITH

"And he saith unto them, Why are ye fearful, O ye of little faith? Then he arose, and rebuked the winds and the sea; and there was a great calm."
Matthew 8:26

Insights:
_____
_____
_____
_____
_____
_____
_____
_____
_____
_____
_____
_____
_____
_____
_____
_____
_____

My Declaration: *"Lord, I declare that **I will not let fear** control my life, but rather I will work on removing all fear and unbelief far from my life."*

FAITH

"But to him that worketh not, but believeth on him that justifieth the ungodly, his faith is counted for righteousness."
Romans 4:5

Insights:

_____
_____
_____
_____
_____
_____
_____
_____
_____
_____
_____
_____
_____
_____
_____
_____
_____
_____
_____

Faith

My Declaration: *"Lord, I declare that my faithfulness and righteousness won't be found in my own abilities. I know that **you are the reason** that I'm saved."*

FAITH

"And Jesus said unto them, Because of your unbelief: for verily I say unto you, If ye have faith as a grain of mustard seed, ye shall say unto this mountain, Remove hence to yonder place; and it shall remove; and nothing shall be impossible unto you."
Matthew 17:20

Insights:
_____
_____
_____
_____
_____
_____
_____
_____
_____
_____
_____
_____
_____
_____
_____
_____
_____
_____

Faith

My Declaration: *"Lord, I declare that I will be fully persuaded in **your ability and promises**. You have the ability to **remove all obstacles** that are in my way."*

FAITH

"And Jesus said unto him, Go thy way; thy faith hath made thee whole. And immediately he received his sight, and followed Jesus in the way."
Mark 10:52

Insights:

_____
_____
_____
_____
_____
_____
_____
_____
_____
_____
_____
_____
_____
_____
_____

My Declaration: "*Lord, I declare that my faith will bring everything that I'm fighting for to completion. I will be made whole because **I have held on tightly to my faith**.*"

FAITH

"If then God so clothe the grass, which is today in the field, and tomorrow is cast into the oven; how much more will he clothe you, O ye of little faith?"
Luke 12:28

Insights:

_____
_____
_____
_____
_____
_____
_____
_____
_____
_____
_____
_____
_____
_____
_____
_____
_____
_____
_____
_____

My Declaration: *"Lord, I declare that I will not look at my circumstances **but I will trust you** in everything I do in life."*

FAITH

"Knowing this, that the trying of your faith worketh patience."
James 1:3

Insights:

Faith

My Declaration: *"Lord, I declare that even though I might find myself in trials,* **I know that you** *are working everything out for my good."*

FAITH

"And Stephen, full of faith and power, did great wonders and miracles among the people."
Acts 6:8

Insights:

_____

_____

_____

_____

_____

_____

_____

_____

_____

_____

_____

_____

_____

_____

_____

_____

_____

_____

My Declaration: "*Lord, I declare that **I will learn** to walk in faith and power. I choose to believe that you will do wonderful things in **my life**.*"

FAITH

*"Who by him do believe in God, that raised him up
from the dead, and gave him glory; that your
faith and hope might be in God."*
1 Peter 1:21

Insights:
_____
_____
_____
_____
_____
_____
_____
_____
_____
_____
_____
_____
_____
_____
_____
_____
_____

Faith

My Declaration: *"Lord, I declare that you have the power to raise me up, even to the point of raising me from the dead. My faith and hope **is in you alone**; I will not lean on myself or my wisdom."*

FAITH

"For therein is the righteousness of God revealed from faith to faith: as it is written, The just shall live by faith."
Romans 1:17

Insights:

_____

_____

_____

_____

_____

_____

_____

_____

_____

_____

_____

_____

_____

_____

_____

_____

_____

_____

_____

Faith

My Declaration: *"Lord, I declare that I will live my life by faith. I will be justified as I continue to walk by faith. My faith will be accounted to me **as being righteous.**"*

FAITH

*"And now abideth faith, hope, charity, these three;
but the greatest of these is charity."*
1 Corinthians 13:13

Insights:

_____
_____
_____
_____
_____
_____
_____
_____
_____
_____
_____
_____
_____
_____
_____
_____
_____
_____

Faith

My Declaration: *"Lord, I declare that I will live my life loving other people. Love is the greatest force on the earth. **My faith works through love.**"*

FAITH

*"Thou art the God that doest wonders:
thou hast declared thy strength among the people."
Psalm 77:14*

Insights:

_____
_____
_____
_____
_____
_____
_____
_____
_____
_____
_____
_____
_____
_____
_____
_____
_____
_____
_____

My Declaration: *"Lord, I declare that **I will remain in faith** until my miracle comes to pass in my life."*

FAITH

"But what saith it? The word is nigh thee, even in thy mouth, and in thy heart: that is, the word of faith, which we preach."
Romans 10:8

Insights:

_____
_____
_____
_____
_____
_____
_____
_____
_____
_____
_____
_____
_____
_____
_____
_____
_____
_____
_____
_____

Faith

My Declaration: *"Lord, I declare that the confession of my mouth will be your word. **I will not allow myself** to become negative. Your word increases my faith."*

FAITH

*"So then faith cometh by hearing,
and hearing by the word of God."
Romans 10:17*

Insights:

_____
_____
_____
_____
_____
_____
_____
_____
_____
_____
_____
_____
_____
_____
_____
_____
_____
_____
_____

Faith

My Declaration: *"Lord, I declare that **I will listen** to your word; I will meditate on it day and night. Faith is coming to me **as I position myself in your word**."*

FAITH

"That your faith should not stand in the wisdom of men, but in the power of God."
1 Corinthians 2:5

Insights:

_____
_____
_____
_____
_____
_____
_____
_____
_____
_____
_____
_____
_____
_____
_____
_____
_____
_____
_____
_____

Faith

My Declaration: *"Lord, I declare that my faith will be found in your wisdom and not in the wisdom of man or myself.* ***Your power will be the strength of my life.****"*

FAITH

*"So then they which be of faith are blessed
with faithful Abraham."*
Galatians 3:9

Insights:

_____

_____

_____

_____

_____

_____

_____

_____

_____

_____

_____

_____

_____

_____

_____

_____

_____

_____

_____

Faith

My Declaration: *"Lord, I declare that your blessings will overtake me. **I will believe your word** that the blessing of the Lord makes me wealthy."*

FAITH

"And Jesus answering saith unto them, Have faith in God."
Mark 11:22

Insights:

_____

_____

_____

_____

_____

_____

_____

_____

_____

_____

_____

_____

_____

_____

_____

_____

_____

_____

_____

Faith

My Declaration: *"Lord, I declare that I will put my trust in you; I will put my confidence **in you alone**."*

FAITH

"For he was a good man, and full of the Holy Ghost and of faith: and much people was added unto the Lord."
Acts 11:24

Insights:
_____
_____
_____
_____
_____
_____
_____
_____
_____
_____
_____
_____
_____
_____
_____
_____
_____

My Declaration: "*Lord, I declare that I will live my life in righteousness. I, too, will tell others about your loving kindness. **My life will be a light to others**.*"

FAITH

"Watch ye, stand fast in the faith, quit you like men, be strong."
1 Corinthians 16:13

Insights:
_____
_____
_____
_____
_____
_____
_____
_____
_____
_____
_____
_____
_____
_____
_____
_____
_____
_____
_____

Faith

My Declaration: *"Lord, I declare that **I will be strong** in difficult circumstances; I will trust you in everything I do in life. I will not quit when things get difficult. **I will stand in faith**."*

FAITH

"By faith Noah, being warned of God of things not seen as yet, moved with fear, prepared an ark to the saving of his house; by the which he condemned the world, and became heir of the righteousness which is by faith."
Hebrews 11:7

Insights:

_____
_____
_____
_____
_____
_____
_____
_____
_____
_____
_____
_____
_____
_____
_____
_____
_____

Faith

My Declaration: *"Lord, I declare that I will listen for your voice and follow your instructions. **I will trust in your ability** as I travel life's journey."*

FAITH

"For ye are all the children of God by faith in Christ Jesus."
Galatians 3:26

Insights:

_____
_____
_____
_____
_____
_____
_____
_____
_____
_____
_____
_____
_____
_____
_____
_____
_____
_____
_____
_____
_____

My Declaration: *"Lord, I declare that I am your child;* ***I live by faith in Jesus Christ.****"*

FAITH

"And the prayer of faith shall save the sick, and the Lord shall raise him up; and if he have committed sins, they shall be forgiven him."
James 5:15

Insights:

_____
_____
_____
_____
_____
_____
_____
_____
_____
_____
_____
_____
_____
_____
_____
_____
_____

My Declaration: *"Lord, I declare that my faith will make me whole; my confidence in you will save me. Your word has power,* ***and it has the ability to heal my body.****"*

FAITH

"But ye, beloved, building up yourselves on your most holy faith, praying in the Holy Ghost ..."
Jude 1:20

Insights:

_____
_____
_____
_____
_____
_____
_____
_____
_____
_____
_____
_____
_____
_____
_____
_____
_____
_____

Faith

My Declaration: *"Lord, I declare that I will pray continually in the Holy Ghost to build myself up. I declare that **I will build myself up through prayer.**"*

FAITH

"And he said, The things which are impossible with men are possible with God."
Luke 18:27

Insights:
_____
_____
_____
_____
_____
_____
_____
_____
_____
_____
_____
_____
_____
_____
_____
_____
_____
_____

My Declaration: *"Lord, I declare that the natural world does not offer the impossible. It will never compare to the limitless power of God. The impossible is only found in my pursuit of God. I will not let natural circumstances ever convince me that there is no hope. Faith is found where the impossible lives, and is **waiting to be released** into my natural circumstances."*

FAITH

"I would seek unto God, and unto God would I commit my cause: Which doeth great things and unsearchable; marvellous things without number: ..."
Job 5:8-9

Insights:
_____
_____
_____
_____
_____
_____
_____
_____
_____
_____
_____
_____
_____
_____
_____
_____
_____

Faith

My Declaration: *"Lord, I declare that I will not put limits on your ability when asking for a miracle;* ***I will believe that you can do the impossible!****"*

FAITH

*"Then touched he their eyes, saying,
According to your faith be it unto you."
Matthew 9:29*

Insights:

Faith

My Declaration: *"Lord, I declare that I will receive the promise of blessing as I place my confidence in you and **as I walk in my faith** and not by sight."*

FAITH

"Flee also youthful lusts: but follow righteousness, faith, charity, peace, with them that call on the Lord out of a pure heart."
2 Timothy 2:22

Insights:

_____
_____
_____
_____
_____
_____
_____
_____
_____
_____
_____
_____
_____
_____
_____
_____
_____

Faith

My Declaration: *"Lord, I declare that I will follow after righteousness.* **I make the choice** *to live out faith and love in my daily life."*

FAITH

"For whatsoever is born of God overcometh the world: and this is the victory that overcometh the world, even our faith."
1 John 5:4

Insights:

_____
_____
_____
_____
_____
_____
_____
_____
_____
_____
_____
_____
_____
_____
_____
_____
_____
_____
_____
_____

My Declaration: *"Lord, I declare that **my faith will overcome** the difficulties I face in life. **You will give me the strength** to carry out the tasks and overcome the obstacles that I face in my life. **I will accomplish the goals** that you have set before me."*

FAITH

*"For as the body without the spirit is dead,
so faith without works is dead also."*
James 2:26

Insights:
_____
_____
_____
_____
_____
_____
_____
_____
_____
_____
_____
_____
_____
_____
_____
_____
_____
_____

Faith

My Declaration: *"Lord, I declare that I will serve you with my whole heart. **I will live out my faith** by doing the work that you have shown me to do."*

FAITH

"Behold, his soul which is lifted up is not upright in him: but the just shall live by his faith."
Habakkuk 2:4

Insights:

_____

_____

_____

_____

_____

_____

_____

_____

_____

_____

_____

_____

_____

_____

_____

_____

_____

Faith

My Declaration: *"Lord, I declare that I will not live my life in pride or in my own strength. I will put my trust and confidence in you **as I live a life of faith**."*

FAITH

"Through faith we understand that the worlds were framed by the word of God, so that things which are seen were not made of things which do appear."
Hebrews 11:3

Insights:
_____
_____
_____
_____
_____
_____
_____
_____
_____
_____
_____
_____
_____
_____
_____
_____
_____
_____

Faith

My Declaration: *"Lord, I declare that I will call those things that are not **as though they are already manifested** in my life."*

FAITH

*"But let him ask in faith, nothing wavering.
For he that wavereth is like a wave of the sea
driven with the wind and tossed."*
James 1:6

Insights:

_____
_____
_____
_____
_____
_____
_____
_____
_____
_____
_____
_____
_____
_____
_____
_____
_____
_____

Faith

My Declaration: *"Lord, I declare that I will not be double minded in my thinking, but I will be fully persuaded by your word: that it is true and that **you are faithful to your word.**"*

FAITH

"For unto us was the gospel preached, as well as unto them: but the word preached did not profit them, not being mixed with faith in them that heard it."
Hebrews 4:2

Insights:

Faith

My Declaration: *"Lord, I declare that as I hear your word, it will have a great effect on my life. I will put my confidence in your word as I hear and obey its truths. As a result,* **I will trust you in everything that I do in life***."*

FAITH

"Beloved, when I gave all diligence to write unto you of the common salvation, it was needful for me to write unto you, and exhort you that ye should earnestly contend for the faith which was once delivered unto the saints."
Jude 1:3

Insights:
_____
_____
_____
_____
_____
_____
_____
_____
_____
_____
_____
_____
_____
_____
_____
_____
_____
_____
_____

Faith

My Declaration: *"Lord, I declare that **I will contend** for the faith that was given to the saints. I will not water down your word to fit my lifestyle, but I will read your word and apply it to my life. **Your word is truth**."*